THIS BOOK

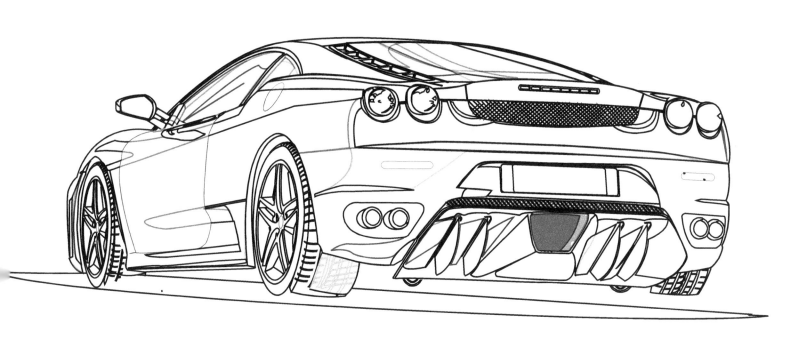

BELONGS TO

○○○○○○○○○○○○

COLOR TEST

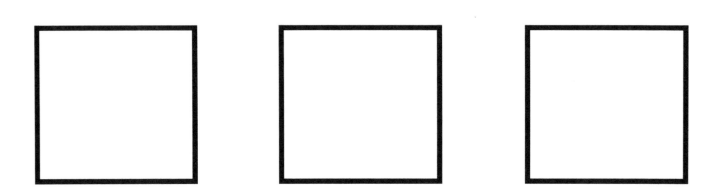

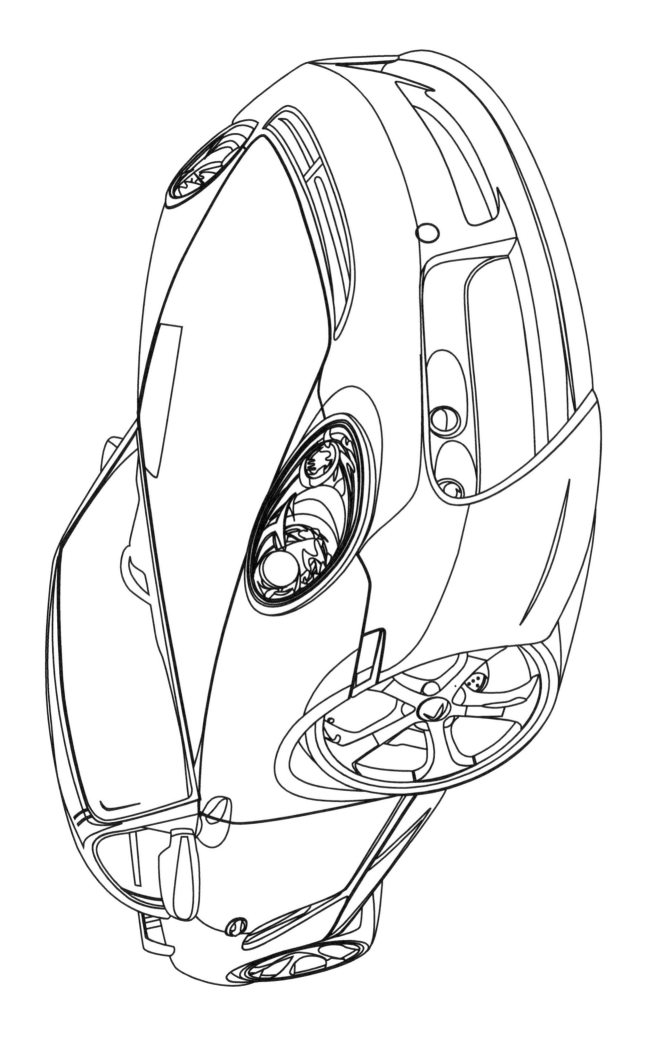

NEXT
SUPER CAR

1

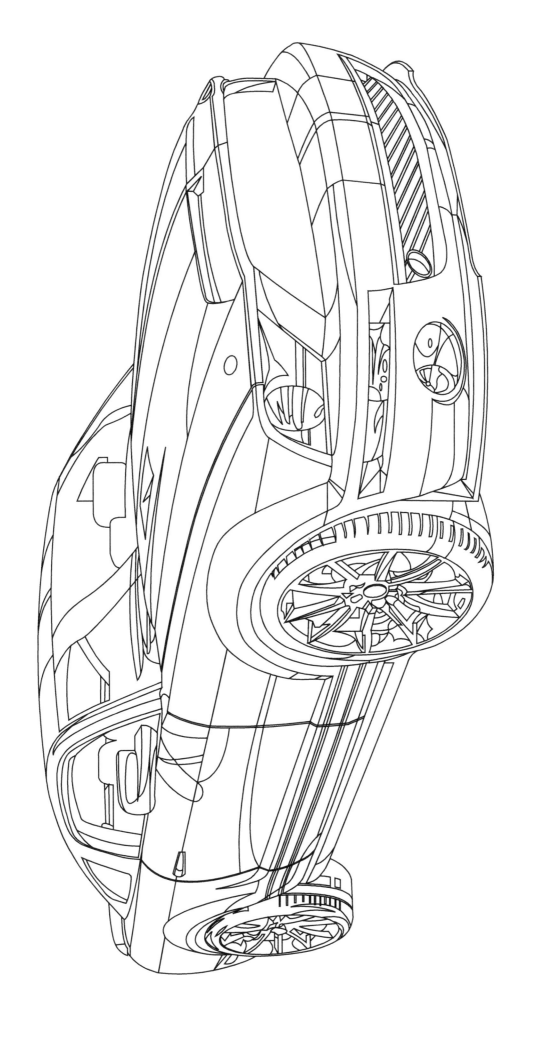

NEXT
SUPER CAR

2

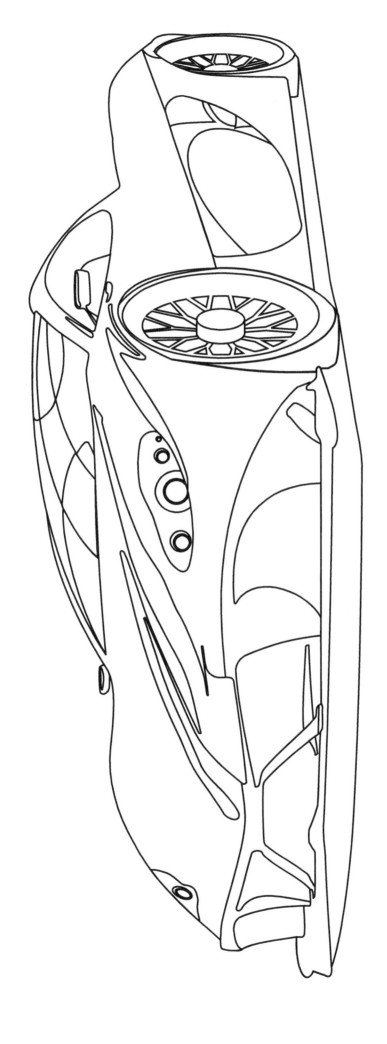

NEXT
SUPER CAR

3

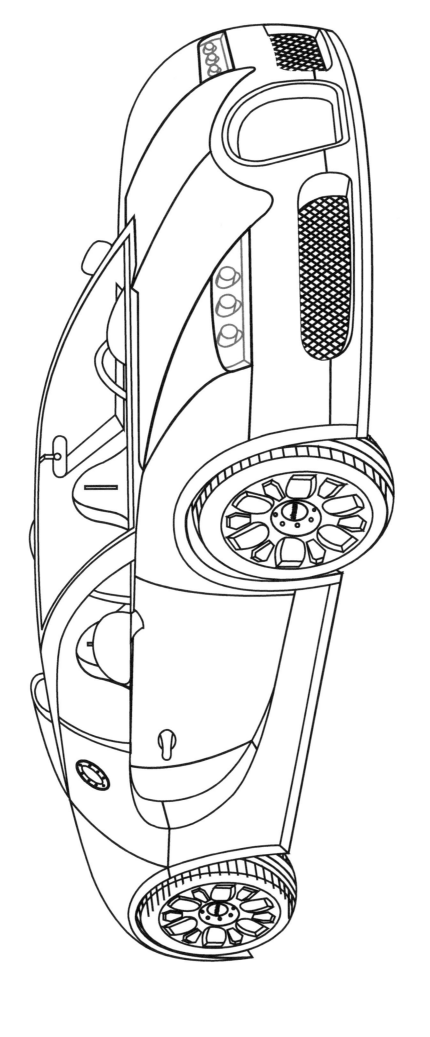

NEXT
SUPER CAR

4

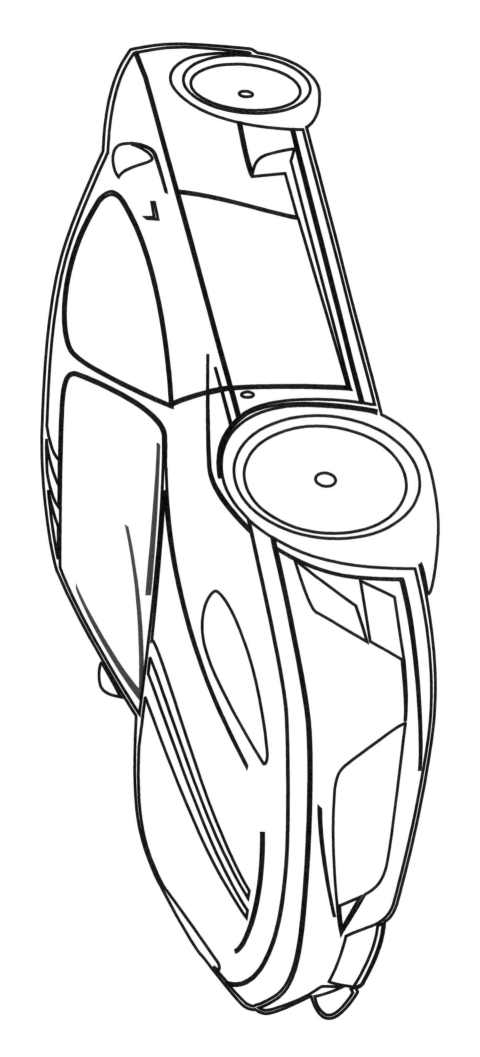

NEXT
SUPER CAR

5

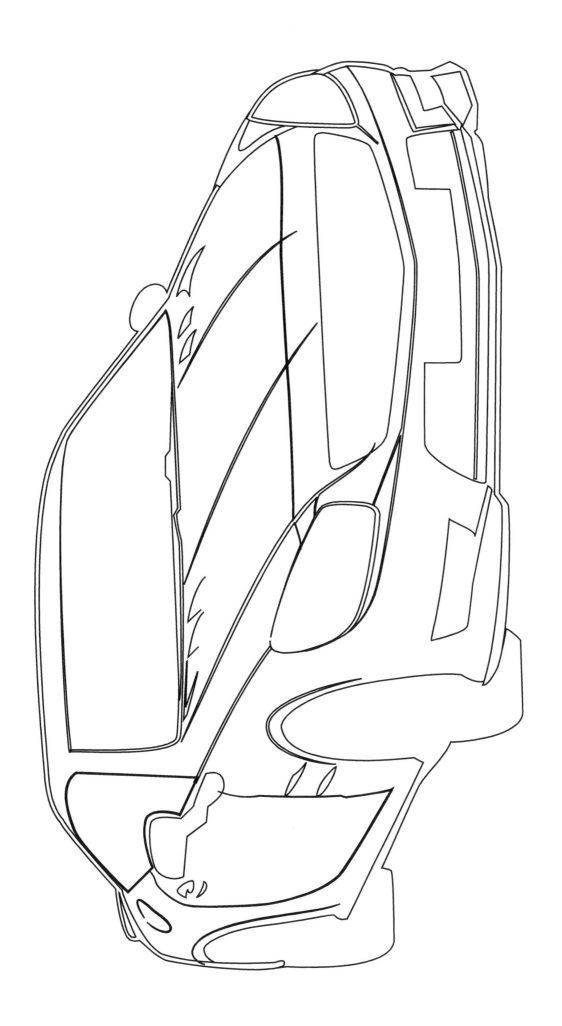

NEXT
SUPER CAR

6

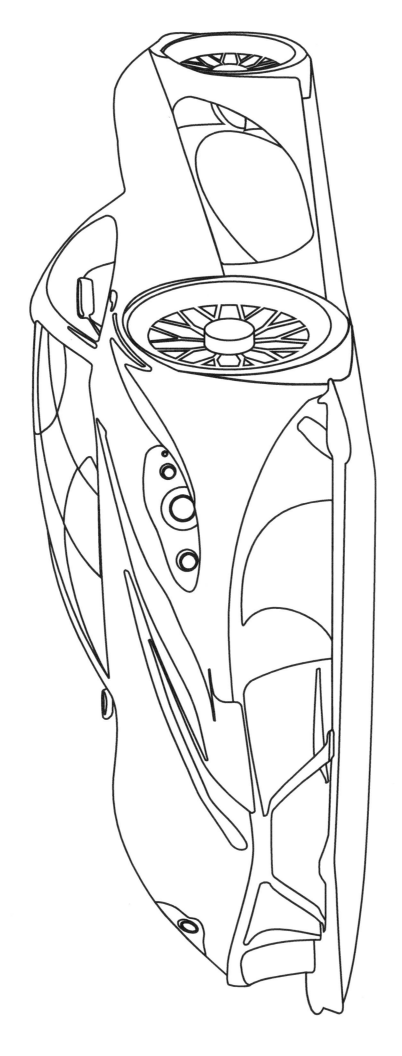

NEXT
SUPER CAR

7

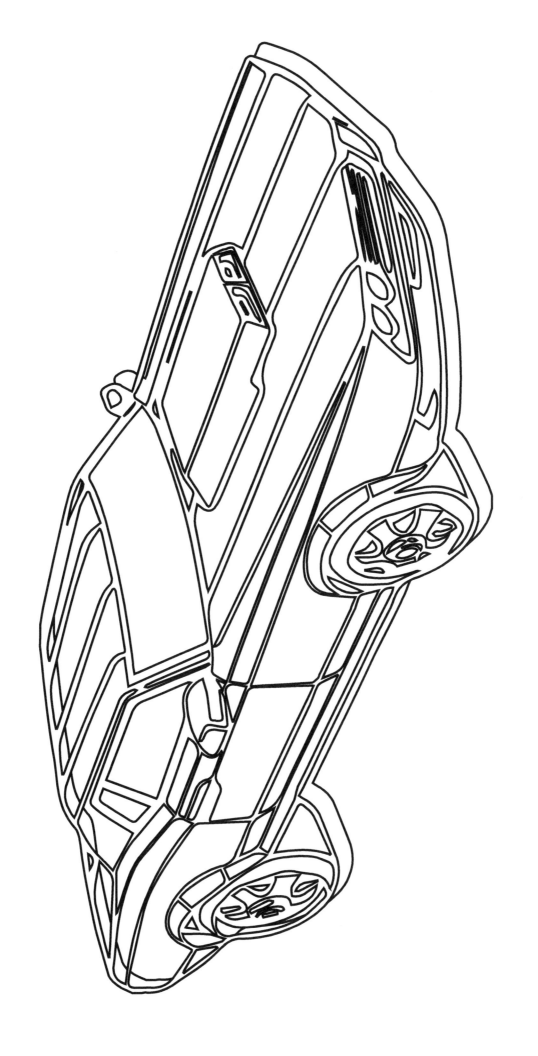

NEXT
SUPER CAR

8

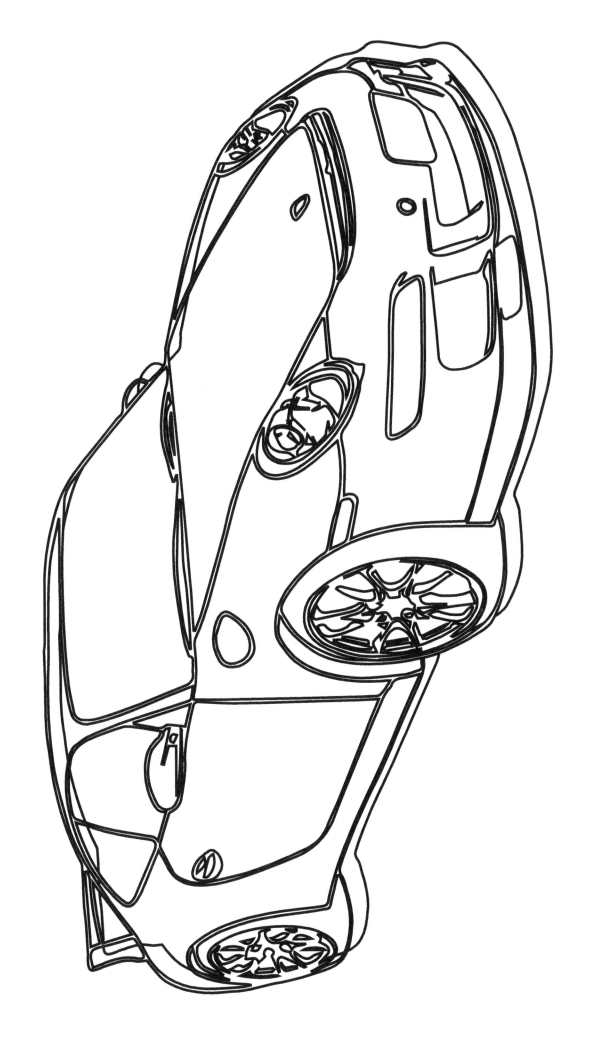

NEXT
SUPER CAR

9

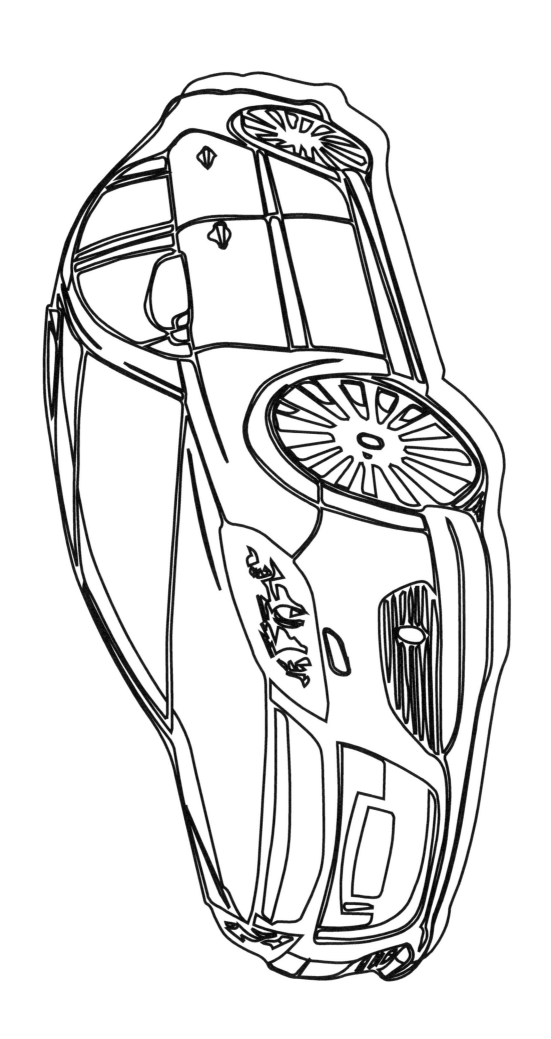

NEXT
SUPER CAR

10

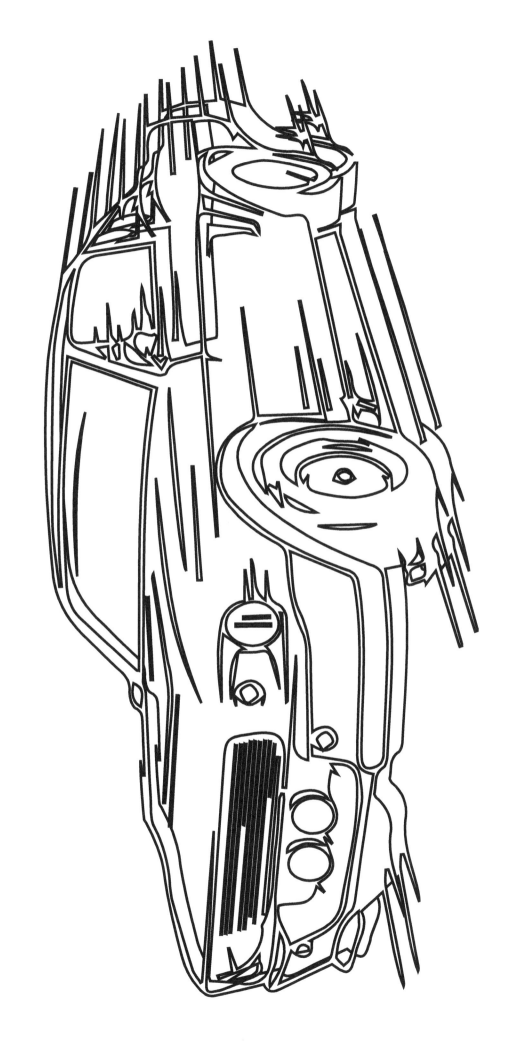

NEXT
SUPER CAR

11

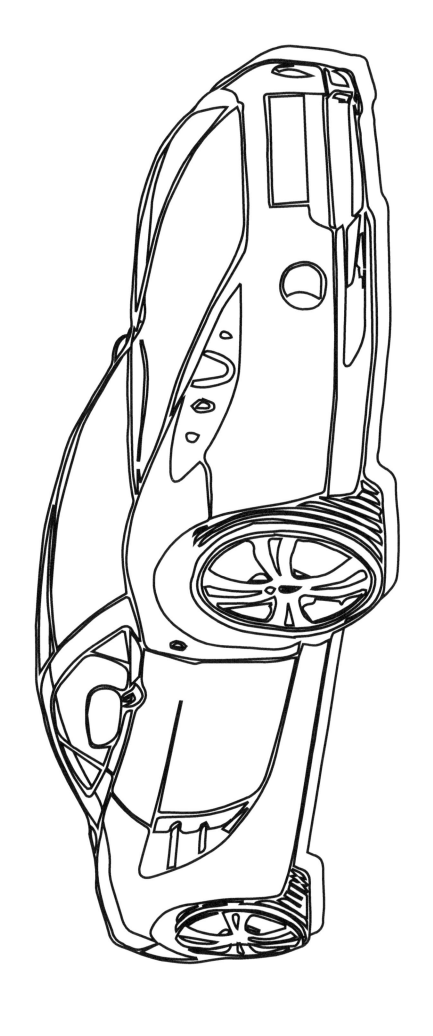

NEXT
SUPER CAR

12

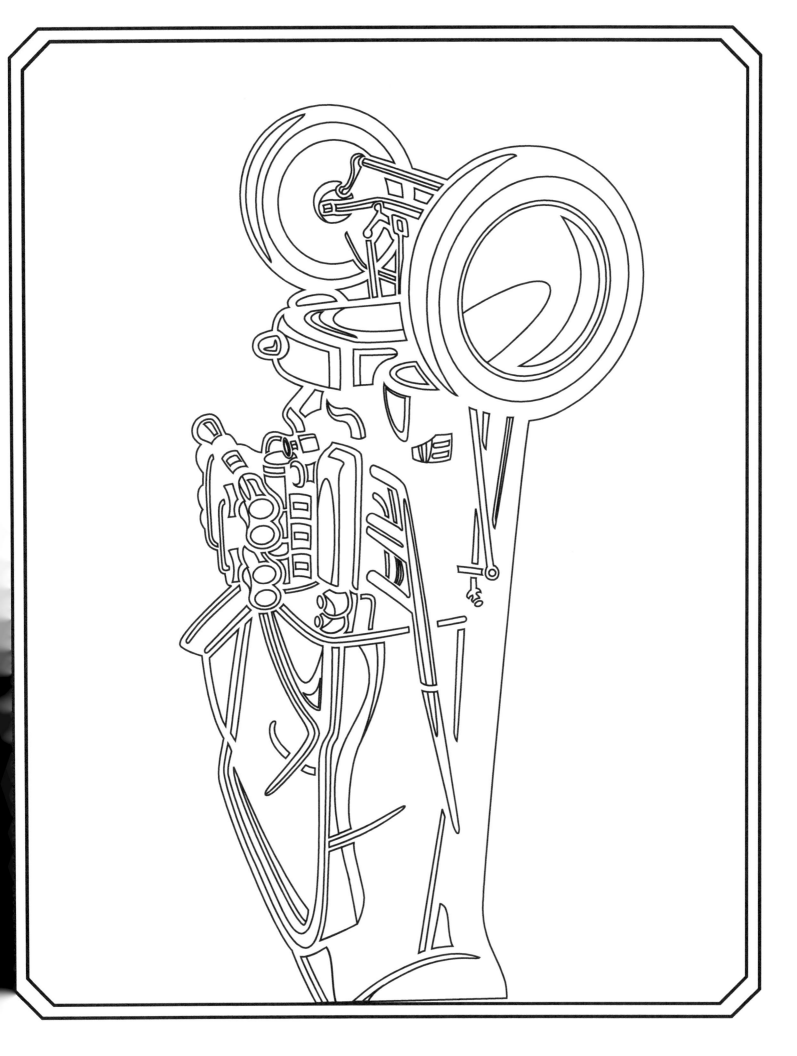

NEXT
SUPER CAR

13

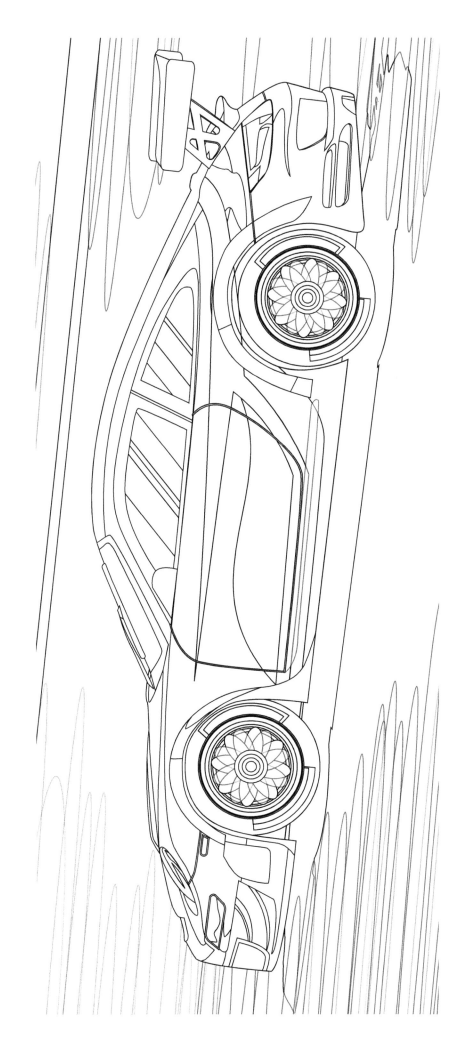

NEXT
SUPER CAR

14

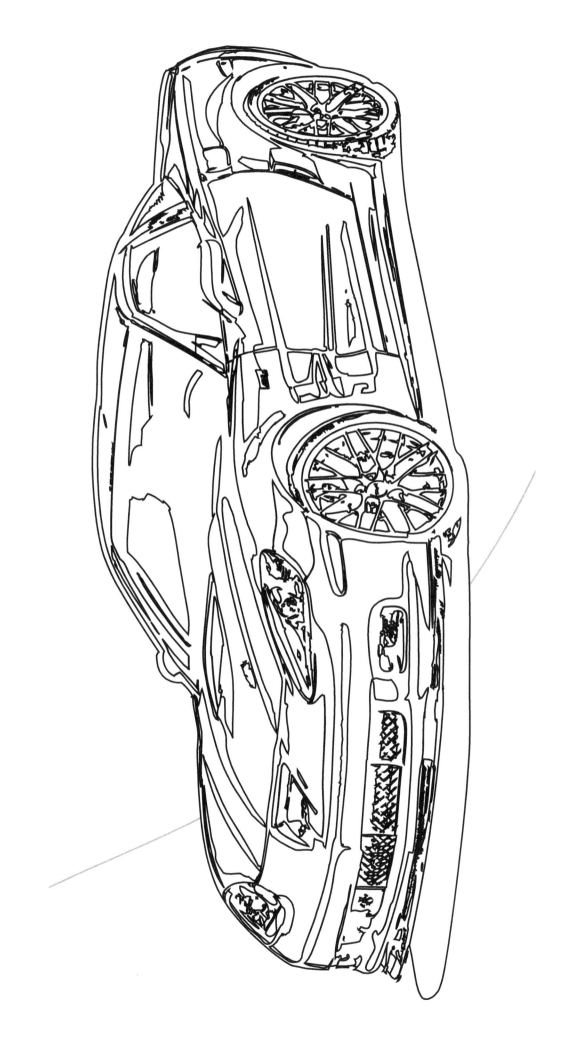

NEXT
SUPER CAR

15

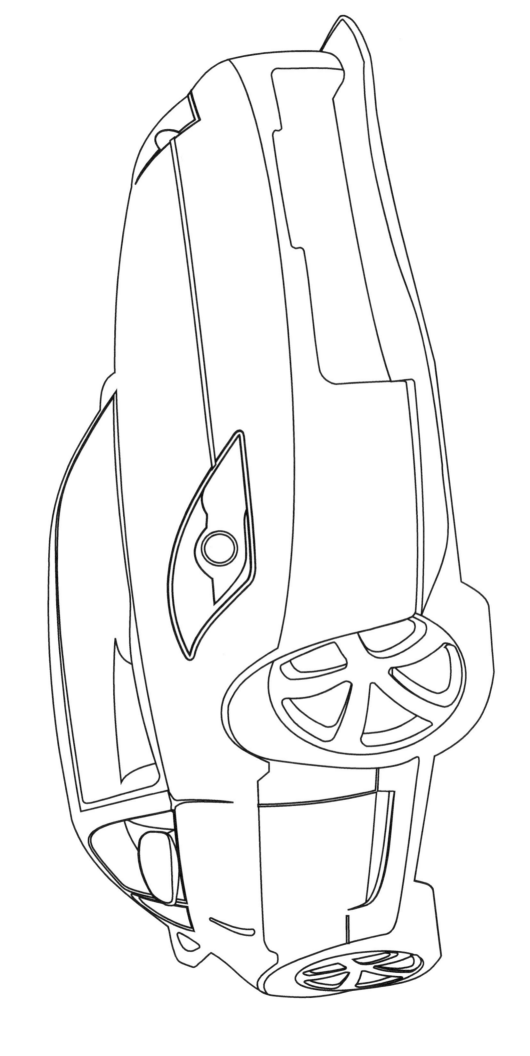

NEXT
SUPER CAR

16

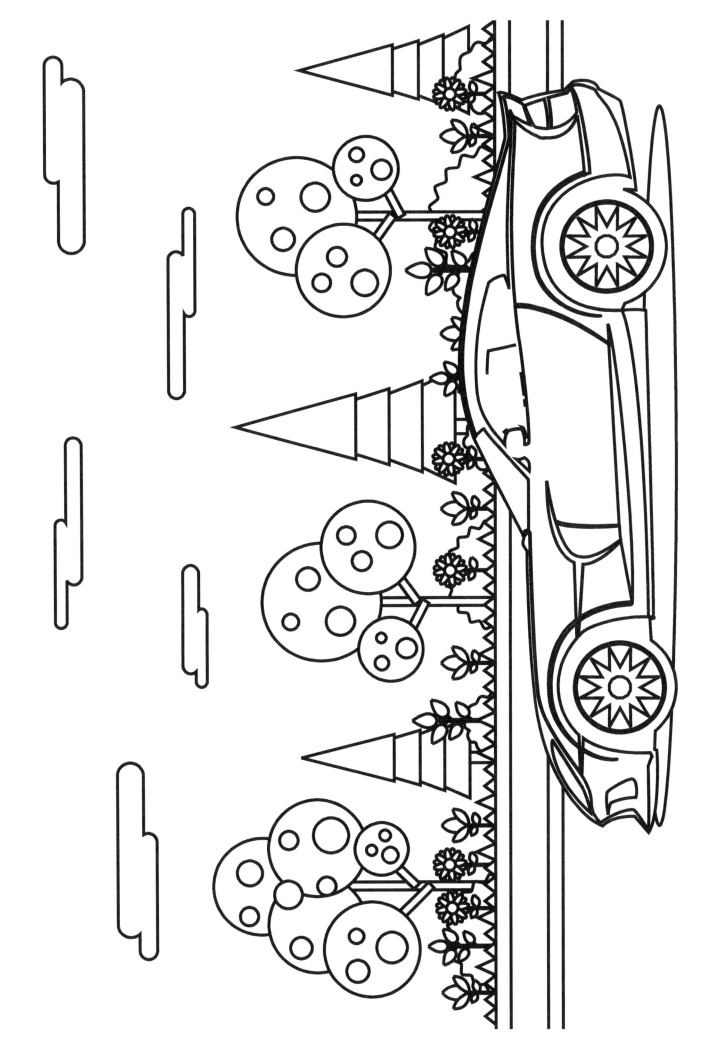

NEXT
SUPER CAR

17

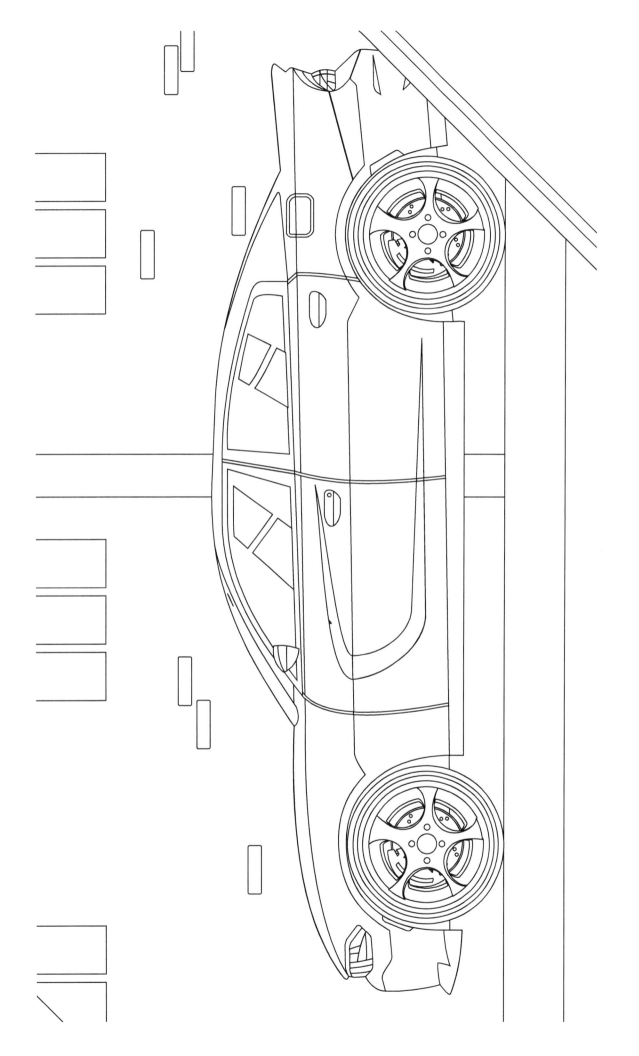

NEXT
SUPER CAR

· · · · · · ·

DRAW YOUR DREAM CAR

www.ingramcontent.com/pod-product-compliance
Lightning Source LLC
LaVergne TN
LVHW082339221224
799685LV00040BC/2217